ON
OUR
FATHER'S
KNEE

ON OUR FATHER'S KNEE

Translated by the author from the original *På Vår Herres fang*

Copyright © 1966 Lutherstiftelsens Forlag, Oslo

Augsburg Paperback, 1973

Library of Congress Catalog Card No. 72-90264

International Standard Book No. 0-8066-1309-2

Manufactured in the United States of America

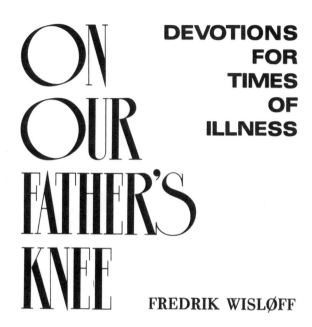

ON OUR FATHER'S KNEE

DEVOTIONS FOR TIMES OF ILLNESS

FREDRIK WISLØFF

Augsburg Publishing House
Minneapolis, Minnesota

To be ill
  is to sit on our Father's knee

To be troubled
  is to feel the Father's embrace

To be in distress
  is to hear the throb of
                the Father's Heart

ON YOUR FATHER'S KNEE

In the morning

> *As one whom his mother comforteth,*
> *so will I comfort you.*   Is. 66:13.

The love of God is just as tender and affectionate, persevering and patient, sympathizing and understanding, — as that of a mother or a father.

You are a child. You are in need of comfort.

And that comfort you will get. Like a loving father, God Himself bends down to you and lifts you up on His knee.

It has been said: «To be ill, is to sit on our Father's knee.»

Through your illness God wants you to learn to become a child again, and so small a child that you are willing to be taken up into your Father's bosom.

He has taken you out of the rough and tumble of life. Now you need to be quiet.

On God's knee you will find *rest*. Here you are to relax, to lay aside everything that is burdening your mind, to forget all your troubles and to rest safe and secure in the presence of God.

Don't let your work, with its demands and duties destroy your peace any longer. Throw yourself onto the bosom of your Heavenly Father and let His arms embrace you.

If you lie still, you will hear the throbbing of His heart. In the whole world no heart is beating for you so tenderly as the heart of God. Every throb echoes the abundance of His love.

Be quiet! Listen!

Feel the loving arms of God and listen to His heart, beating for you.

At noon

Into a home, death came as an uninvited guest, and took one of the children, leaving sorrow and loss.

No one grieved like the mother.

One day the minister met her and tried to comfort her.

«Don't grieve so deeply, mother,» he said. «Take it more philosophically — think of the seven children you still have. Now that the eighth one has gone there is one mouth less to feed and one body less to clothe.»

But the mother looked at the minister, and, shaking her head sadly, answered:

«You know very little of the heart of a mother, Sir, if you can speak like that. Having eight children, she has eight rooms in her heart. When she loses one of them, the seven others can never fill the empty place left by the one who has gone.»

Such is the heart of God.

Even you have a special room in the heart of your Heavenly Father. His love is for *you;* no other can take your place.

Yield yourself to Him to-day and you will find that He holds you in His arms.

The poem of the day

«Sit still, my daughter! Just sit calmly still!
Nor deem these days — these waiting days — as ill!
The One Who loves thee best, Who plans thy way,

Has not forgotten thy great need to-day!
And, if He waits, 'tis sure He waits to prove
To thee, His tender child, His heart's deep love.»

«Sit still, my daughter! Just sit calmly still!
Nor move one step, not even one, until
His way hath opened. Then, ah then, how sweet!
How glad thy heart, and then how swift thy feet
Thy inner being then, ah then, how strong!
And waiting days not counted then too long.»

«Sit still, my daughter! Just sit calmly still!
What higher service could'st thou for Him fill?
'Tis hard! ah yes! But choicest things must cost!
For lack of losing all how much is lost!
'Tis hard, 'tis true! But then — He giveth grace
To count the hardest spot the sweetest place.»

In the evening

Fear thou not!
Let not thy hands be slack!
The Lord thy God in the midst of thee is mighty;
He will save; He will rejoice over thee with joy;

He will rest in His love; He will joy over thee with singing. Zeph. 3:16/17.

Do not think that God is angry. It may seem to you as though God is passive, that He is doing nothing to give you relief. But He has not forgotten you: «*He rests in His love.*»

God has not left you alone. «*The Lord thy God, in the midst of thee is mighty; He will save.*»

He does not think of you with indignation. His look is not one of reproach. «*He will rejoice over thee with joy; He will joy over thee with singing.*»

Be of good cheer — You have a tender and loving Father.

Go to sleep confident and at rest. God Himself will watch over you.

Sleep in the Name of Jesus as securely as a child in his mother's arms.

FROM WHENCE COMETH
MY HELP?

In the morning

> *And the word of the Lord came unto Elijah saying: Get thee hence, and turn thee eastward, and hide thyself by the brook Cherith. And it shall be that thou shall drink of the brook; and I have commanded the ravens to feed thee there.*   I Kings 17:2/4.

The people of Israel are facing a time of great trial. God is sending drought and famine all through the land. But for His faithful servant God has prepared a hiding-place. Down by the brook Cherith, there the Lord Himself will take care of him.

What love God has for His own! In times of difficulty He will never fail to find a safe hiding-place for His children. The Lord never forgets His own. But He uses strange messengers to bring food to Elijah — He sends ravens. By the will of God, those ugly, greedy, black birds have to serve His child. At another time Elijah would have driven them away. Now he knows that God has taken them into His service. Morning and evening he lifts his head to listen. When he hears the sound of the ravens' wings it seems to him a message carried by angels.

Do not fear that which seems dark and devouring. All that touches the life of a Christian, even if it seems untoward, is made to serve the will of God. And God has but one purpose: the good of His children.

That which seems dark and dreary is in truth the gleaming wings of angels. Your lonely little Cherith will become a holy place to you. There you will experience day by day the father-care of God. So put away your sorrow. God has promised to take care of you.

You will not always stay by Cherith. But as long as you remain there, God Himself will enclose you in His love, on hidden wings He will send you His richest gifts.

At noon

Now you are going to translate what you read this morning, in terms of your own life.

Elijah — is yourself.

Cherith — is the place where you are now.

The ravens — are your troubles and difficulties.

Just as God led Elijah, so He will guide you. Has He ever forsaken you?

When hard experiences came you were frightened. You seemed to be facing something evil and uncanny. You saw the black wings of birds of prey that came to rob you. You thought they would steal your health, wreck your future, take your dear ones and leave you alone, sorrowing and bereft. When the black birds came, you thought your peace and happiness would fly away.

But what have you found? The black birds did not come to rob you. They came with blessings from God. In their beaks they had gifts from your Heavenly Father. When the birds left, you were richer than ever before.

Do not be afraid of «bad things». God never gives anything bad to His children. That which

God sends or which He allows to come, is always
for good, even if it is brought to you on black
wings.

The poem of the day

Called aside —
From the glad working of thy busy life,
From the world's ceaseless stir of care and strife,
Into the shade and stillness by thy Heavenly Guide
For a brief space thou hast been called aside.

Called aside —
Perhaps into a desert garden dim;
Yet not alone, when thou hast been with Him,
And heard His Voice in sweetest accents say:
«Child, wilt thou not with Me this still hour stay?»

Called aside —
In hidden paths with Christ thy Lord to tread,
Deeper to drink at the sweet Fountainhead,
Closer in fellowship with Him to roam,
Nearer perchance, to feel thy Heavenly Home.

Called aside —
Oh, restful thought — He doeth all things well;

Oh, blessed sense, with Christ alone to dwell;
So in the shadow of Thy cross to hide,
We thank Thee, Lord, to have been called aside.

In the evening

I will lift up mine eyes unto the mountains:
From whence shall my help come?
My help cometh from the Lord,
Who made heaven and earth.
He will not suffer thy foot to be moved:
He that keepeth thee will not slumber.
Behold, He that keepeth Israel will neither slum-
ber nor sleep.
The Lord is thy keeper:
The Lord is thy shade upon thy right hand.
The sun shall not smite thee by day, nor the
moon by night.
The Lord will keep thee from all evil:
He will keep thy soul.
The Lord will keep thy going out and thy
coming in
From this time and for evermore.   Psalm 121.

*

Now I lay me down to sleep,
I pray Thee, Lord, my soul to keep.
If I should die before I wake,
I pray Thee, Lord, my soul to take.
If I shall live through other days,
I pray Thee, Lord, to guide my ways.

                              Amen.

BITTERNESS

In the morning

> *Behold, it was for my peace that I had
> great bitterness.*   Is. 38:17.

In everybody's life there is something bitter.
Everyone is given the cup of joy, but each one
finds it is mingled with drops of bitterness.

Confronted with the cup of suffering, every
man is put to his hardest test: will the bitter taste
cause bitterness in his heart?

Bitterness is a protest against destiny. Therefore,
bitterness is a protest against God.

The man who becomes bitter, loses peace of heart.
Bitterness always brings with it restlessness, anguish
and pain.

Bitterness makes the bitter drops still more bitter.

But God desires to change bitterness into peace.

«Behold, it was for my peace that I had great bitterness.»

Bitterness dwells in the heart which is protesting. Peace dwells in the heart which is humble before God.

Stop your protests, so bitterness will become peace.

No one has drunk such a bitter cup as Jesus. Though He prayed: «My Father, if it be possible let this cup pass away from Me,» yet He added humbly: «Nevertheless, not as I will, but as Thou wilt.» The bitter cup He emptied became a fountain of peace for countless sinners who believe in Him.

Bow low and lay your will under the hand of God. Drink your cup without protest. The bitterness will be transformed into peace.

Do not compare your bitter draught with the cup that others have to drink. Every one has his share of suffering, though none may see it. Rather consider the bitter cup which Jesus drank to the dregs in your place.

Do not upbraid God. Do not blame Him for these hard happenings. Do not even ask: *why*.

God will not give you more bitter drops than

He sees you need. He will strengthen you to empty your cup.

«And in that day thou shalt say, I will give thanks unto Thee, O Jehovah; for though Thou wast angry with me, Thine anger is turned away, and Thou comfortest me.» Is. 12:1.

At noon

Away in a lonely spot in Norway, in a little home for aged people, lived an old woman who suffered from an eye-disease.

Every morning the matron had to put three drops into her eyes. The drops, however, were bitter and the eyes of the old woman were intensely painful.

«Leave me alone,» she often said. «I won't have those drops. They hurt me.»

One day the Norwegian Crown Prince Olaf was passing through the district, and it was suggested he should pay a visit to the old people's home.

Those were busy days. The house had to be cleaned all over, and the old people found their best clothes.

The day came when the Crown Prince was expected.

The matron was so busy that she forgot the old lady's eyes.

But the old woman remembered it herself:

«Matron dear, are you not coming to put the drops in my eyes? Don't forget me. You must put many drops in today. I want to see the King's son very clearly.»

— — —

That is why God is giving you the bitter drops. His purpose is that you shall see the Son of the Heavenly King clearly. Your eyes need to be brightened.

The poem of the day

> The dark brown mould's upturned
> By the sharp-pointed plow;
> And I've a lesson learned.
>
> My life is but a field.
> Streched out beneath God's sky,
> Some harvest rich to yield.

Where grows the golden grain?
Where faith? Where sympathy?
In a furrow cut by pain.

In the evening

«*When Jesus therefore had received the vinegar, He said, It is finished.*» John 19:30.

In that way the reconciliation was made.
First: the vinegar. And then a finished salvation.
First: the bitter drops, and then peace.
Now, however, peace is obtained. Jesus has done everything as your substitute.
«*It is finished!*»
Give Him thanks and the whole of salvation is yours.

BE GOOD

In the morning

> *«Even so let your light shine before men; that they may see your good works, and glorify your Father Who is in heaven.»*   Matt. 5:16.

In this dark world there is no more light than that which comes from the Christians. «Ye are the Light of the world.» If this light becomes darkness, how great is that darkness!

So let your light be shining!

The light of the Christians is their *good works.* We are not saved by good works; from the Heavenly standpoint no act is good unless it springs from a mind which is born of God.

But being born of God, the new mind will naturally express itself in good works.

To be sanctified is to be good. And this goodness is the light which shines out from a child of God.

The world is longing to see truly good men who are possessed by God, those who are kind, ready to help, patient, indulgent, men who have a kind word for those who are crossing their ways, and a cheerful spirit that makes other people happy.

The ill-humoured man who is irritable, critical, egoistical, brings no light from God to other people.

Ask God to give you the right attitude. You know how encouraging it is to meet kind people. Don't be among those who are expecting other people to be good to them. Be kind yourself, — never mind how other people act.

In that way your own life will be enriched and your light will shine before men, so they will learn to glorify your Father Who is in heaven.

At noon

In 1858 the Crimean War broke out. The war was bloody and hard, accompanied by terrible sufferings for thousands of wounded and sick soldiers.

The hospital service was in disorder, and there were no nurses.

At that time, a noble English lady, Florence Nightingale, left for Crimea, accompanied by thirty-eight young women. The British Minister of War gave Florence Nightingale absolute authority to organize the hospital service in the field. And Florence and her friends took up the work. Wherever these women went, they relieved suffering, bound up wounds, and spread love and light. The air became purer when they entered.

Florence herself worked at Scutari hospital. The soldiers called her: «the lady with the lamp». At night she usually walked among the beds, carrying her little lamp in her hand, and the soldiers would try to stay awake until she came in order to get a glimpse of her. It was said of Florence Nightingale: «She belongs to a sect that — alas — is very small, namely, that of the Good Samaritan.»

That «sect» all Christians should join, — even you in your bed of sickness. Be the light of God to everyone who sees you.

*

The poem of the day

«Follow Me, and I will make you» ...
Make you speak My words with power,
Make you channels of My mercy,
Make you helpful every hour.

«Follow Me, and I will make you» ...
Make you what you cannot be —
Make you loving, trustful, godly,
Make you even like to Me.

In the evening

And if I bestow all my goods to feed the poor, and if I give my body to be burned, but have not love, it profiteth me nothing. Love suffereth long, and is kind; love envieth not; love vaunteth not itself, is not puffed up, doth not behave itself unseemly, seeketh not its own, is not provoked, taketh not account of evil; rejoiceth not in unrighteousness, but rejoiceth with the truth; beareth all things, believeth all things, hopeth all things, endureth all things.

Love never faileth: but whether there be pro-

*phecies, they shall be done away; whether there be
tongues, they shall cease; whether there be know-
ledge, it shall be done away.* I. Cor. 13:3/8.

How may we increase in this love?
Scripture says:
«We love Him, because He first loved us.»
«To whom little is forgiven, the same loveth
little.» Great grace works great love.

Rest in the sunshine of God's love. Remember
and consider what He has given to you: the forgiveness of your sins. How can you but love Him!

NOT PENALTY BUT GRACE

In the morning

> *«Master, who sinned, this man, or his parents, that he should be born blind?» Jesus answered: «Neither did this man sin, nor his parents: but that the works of God should be made manifest in him.»* John 9:2/3.

The disciples were all sure of one thing. This man's illness certainly must be a judgment of God on his sin. But it would be interesting to know whether the sin was his own or the parents'.

The theory that sickness is punishment for sin is still common. Consciously or unconsciously most people think so, not least the sufferer. The sick man thinks that God had to take him aside in order to punish him. His life has not been as it ought to have been. He was not worthy to remain in his work any longer. God had to stop him. The sins which he has committed have caused his sickness.

Sick people may think in this way. But it is not right.

It is true that neither life nor work has been as it ought to be, and that God will indeed sanctify you now through your sickness.

It is *not* true, however, that the sickness has been sent you as a punishment for sin. «Neither has this man sinned nor his parents —», Jesus says.

Do not consider your sickness as a punishment. It is not true. Your sickness has been given to you as a gift from your Heavenly Father. It is given in love and concern.

Through your sickness «*the works of God shall be manifest in you.*» God Himself will reveal His glory; both to you and to your dear ones, therefore your sickness is not punishment, but grace.

«We know that all things work together for good to them that love God.»

At noon

The Dome of Invalids in Paris is erected to commemorate those who have suffered for their country.

In this dome there is an altar. Behind the altar

there are windows made of golden glass, and through these windows the light shines in with golden splendour. Even on dark, cloudy days it is like sunlight shining on the altar.

The whole world is like a great Dome of Invalids.

Every living man is suffering. Each one has an altar where willingly or of necessity he has to bring his sacrifices.

A child of God, however, is in a privileged position. Over his altar the sun of God is shining. Even on dark, cloudy days, in adversity and distress, the light of eternal hope is flooding his life. He acknowledges that God has allowed the sufferings of his life and the conciousness of that is like a golden window through which the sun is always shining.

The poem of the day

It is the branch that bears the fruit
That feels the knife,
To prune it for a larger growth,
A fuller life.

Though every budding twig be lopped,
And every grace

Of swaying tendril, springing leaf,
Be lost a space.

Rejoice, tho' each desire, each dream,
Each hope of thine
Shall fall and fade; it is the hand
of Love Divine

That holds the knife, that cuts and breaks
With tenderest touch,
That thou, whose life has borne some fruit
May'st now bear much.

In the evening

My son, regard not lightly the chastening of the
Lord,
   Nor faint when thou art reproved of Him;
   For whom the Lord loveth He chasteneth,
   And scourgeth every son whom He receiveth.
Heb. 12:5/6.

«Do not faint,» the Lord says.
If you feel God's chastening, then know:
1). It is because you are a child of God, He is

chastening you. He will not leave you to go on your way alone; He will take care of you.

2). The chastening is an expression of love. Therefore He sets limits to His chastening. In these days you are getting exactly what you need.

3). «He is chastening you for your profit, that you might be partaker of His holiness.» Therefore you may rejoice. Nothing is more profitable than to be partaker of His holiness.

Do not faint, but rejoice.

THE SERVICE OF INTERCESSION

In the morning

> *The Lord turned the captivity of Job when he prayed for his friends: also the Lord gave Job twice as much as he had before.* Job. 42:10.

The friends caused Job much pain. They did not mean to trouble him. What they said to Job was partly true, but they twisted the words round in such a way that Job was tempted to reason with God.

Often Job must have wished that his friends would be quiet and leave him. They and their words were tiring him.

Job, however, conquered himself.

He won the victory by prayer. Instead of blaming his friends and growing bitter, he prayed for them.

And by this intercession, blessing returned to Job himself. *«The Lord turned the captivity of Job when he prayed for his friends: also the Lord gave Job twice as much as he had before.»*

Have you experienced the blessings of intercession?

They are twofold.

By your prayer, the grace of God is poured out on the one for whom you are praying. Consider how much other people lose when we do not pray for them.

At the same time, the blessing returns to the one who is praying. If you pray for only a few people, you will be spiritually poor yourself. We are all tempted to become selfcentered. It appears very often in our prayers. They are centered just around ourselves, consequently, we find little enjoyment in our life of prayer, and so we get tired.

But there is a way out of this.

Pray more for other people, and you will rejoice accordingly. Become an eager intercessor and your whole life of prayer will become fruitful.

If you are centered only in yourself, your suffering will become still greater. If you dedicate yourself to prayer for other people, God will deliver you from your tribulations, recompensing you with blessings.

At noon

Intercession is the fruit of Christian love. Little intercession is caused by little love.

Intercession is prayer in the guise of service.

Intercession is opening the windows of our small chamber, looking out to the very end of the world.

Intercession saves the one who is making it from self-centred prayer.

Intercession gives prayer a scheme and a goal.

Intercession makes prayer exciting and expectant.

Intercession is the best favour to a friend. If you want to know how many friends you have, just count how many you are praying for.

Intercession's greatest triumph is prayer for enemies.

Intercession means conquest of aversion and of ill-will.

Intercession is the training-school of all Christian activity. Having started to pray for a man, you will be obliged to testify to him. By praying the Lord of the harvest that He will send forth labourers, you will soon be at work in His harvest-field yourself.

Intercession saves from cold routine.

Intercession is the last means of work that will be taken out of the hands of God's people. No prohibition of an ungodly ruler can hinder us from intercession.

Intercession is the hope of the world. As long as a man has an intercessor, he may hope to be saved.

Intercession is moving the arm of Almighty God.

Intercession means the death of spiritual indolence.

Intercession comes back to the one who prays with blessings and happiness.

Intercession's greatest service takes place at the throne of God, where the Heavenly High-Priest Himself, is revealed as the Intercessor of the whole world.

The poem of the day

«Stir me, oh, stir me, Lord, I care not how,
But stir my heart in passion for the world,
Stir me to give, to go, but most to pray;
Stir, till the blood-red banner be unfurled
O'er lands that still in heathen darkness lie,
O'er deserts where no cross is lifted high.»

«Stir me, oh! stir me, Lord, till all my heart
Is filled with strong compassion for these souls;
Till Thy compelling word drives me to pray;
Till Thy constraining love reach to the poles
Far north and south, in burning deep desire,
Till east and west are caught in love's great fire.»

«Stir me, oh, stir me, Lord, till prayer is pain,
Till prayer is joy, till prayer turns into praise;
Stir me, till heart and will and mind, yea, all
Is wholly Thine to use through all the days.
Stir, till I learn to pray exceedingly;
Stir, till I learn to wait expectantly.»

B. P. Head.

In the evening

And in like manner the Spirit also helpeth our infirmity: for we know not how to pray as we ought; but the Spirit Himself maketh intercession for us with groanings which cannot be uttered; and He that searcheth the heart knoweth what is in the mind of the Spirit, because He makes intercession for the saints according to the will of God.

Rom. 8:26/27.

I thank Thee, Thou Holy Spirit, Thou my Helper, for making intercession for me. I myself am feeble in prayer and weak in intercession. I thank Thee, because Thou are praying for me, in spite of that. Lord, I am in need of Thine intercession. Help my infirmity. Thy prayers are always answered, for Thou art praying according to the will of God.

I thank Thee for this day, and I beg Thee, make even me a better intercessor.

Amen.

BLESS THE LORD, O MY SOUL

In the morning

> *Bless the Lord, O my soul; and forget not all His benefits: Who forgiveth all thine iniquities; Who healeth all thy diseases.* Ps. 103:2/3.

Make your sick bed an altar where you bring sacrifices of thanks unto God. Let these days of sickness be occupied with praise and singing unto God.

Thousands have done it before you; now they are looking back to their experience of sickness as a rich time of joy.

«*Forget not all His benefits.*»

Consider them, one by one.

First, look back at the time when you were well. Begin by thanking God for it.

Then take your illness, these days which you now experience. Consider from what you have been spared and how well He has taken care of you in the past.

It is strange that all the good things we have received from God are so easily forgotten. We remember the troubles and distresses; the benefits of God we forget.

«He forgiveth all thine iniquities.»

All thine iniquities!

God repays iniquities with benefits!

Then we certainly ought to thank Him.

«Bless the Lord, O my soul:» Forgiveness of sins is an inexhaustible fountain of joy. Seeing the privilege of possessing the grace of God, joy will always be the dominant note of the soul's hymn.

«He healeth all thy diseases.»

Even your disease is in the Hand of your Father. When God's time has come, He will heal you. And until that day He will make all the bad things work for your good.

Yes indeed! Bless the Lord, O my soul.

Make your little bedroom a chapel of praise.

*

At noon

Turgenjew, the Russian author, tells this allegory:
God once had invited all the virtues to a party
in Heaven.

They all came and rejoiced to see one another.

At the table, two of them, both strangers to each
other, happened to sit side by side, and so God had
to introduce them. The one was *Charity,* and the
other *Gratitude.*

Such is the story.

It is not charity that makes men happy, but
gratitude. Heaven is full of thanks. We have got
as much of Heaven on earth as we have learned to
give thanks.

In his book, «Happy-Peter», Hendrik Pontoppi-
dan tells this incident about the young Jewish girl
who was a «freethinker». She walked in the garden,
happy in her mind, carrying a letter in her hand.
The letter had come from her sweetheart saying
that he was on his way to her. Then, «for the first
time in her life, she missed a god before whom she
could kneel down, and to whom she could give
thanks.»

People never miss God as much as in great tribulations and in great happiness.

If you believe in God, lift up your heart to Him and praise Him.

The poem of the day

Sing a little song of trust,
O my heart!
Sing it just because you must,
As leaves start;
As flowers push their way through dust;
Sing, my heart, because you must!

Wait not for an eager throng —
Bird on bird;
'Tis the solitary song
That is heard.
Every voice at dawn will start,
Be a nightingale, my heart!

Sing across the winter snow,
Pierce the cloud;
Sing when mists are drooping low —

Clear and loud;
But sing sweetest in the dark:
He who slumbers not will hark.

In the evening

After these things I saw, and behold, a great multitude, which no man could number, out of every nation and of all tribes and people and tongues, standing before the throne and before the Lamb, arrayed in white robes, and palms in their hands; and they cry with a great voice, saying, Salvation unto our God Who sitteth on the throne, and unto the Lamb. And all the angels were standing round about the throne, and about the elders and the four living creatures; and they fell before the throne on their faces, and worshipped God, saying,

Amen: Blessing, and glory, and wisdom, and thanksgiving, and honor, and power, and might, be unto our God for ever and ever. Amen.

Rev. 7:9/12.

That which unites the great white multitude in Heaven with God, is gratitude and praise.

See that you too are united with God through thanksgiving.

Thereby will you be united with the heavenly multitude as well.

Close this day giving thanks unto God, and so you will sleep safely.

Goodnight, in the name of Jesus.

NOT I, BUT JESUS

In the morning

> *I have been crucified with Christ; and it is no longer I that live, but Christ liveth in me.*   Gal. 2:20.

«It is no longer I that live.» That is the position of a Christian. My own ego has been given to death. Not only is it true that Christ has died for me; I have also died with Christ.

The old Adam with his inclinations and desires has been crucified. Every time the old desires awaken, they must be put to death. The ego has no rights any more. It still claims to be considered, it wants to be cared for and to have its own way, but its claims have no rights. The ego is to be trampled on and put to death. «I die daily,» Paul says. (I Cor. 15:31.)

This is the suffering that accompanies all sanctification. No one who wishes to live in Christ can be without it.

But this is also the blessedness of the Christian life. There is no flood of real joy from the satisfaction of the flesh. If you want to be happy, your ego has to die. God never wants to hurt you; all your pain comes from your own will.

The more you follow the claim of your ego, the more empty and painful will your life become. The more your ego is put to death, the happier you will be.

«It is no longer I that live, but Christ liveth in me.»

As a Christian you have got a new ego, — that is Christ. He decides for you what to do, and He directs you and lives in you. The life of Christ is your life. His peace and joy are yours.

«*Christ liveth in me.*»

At noon

A North-Indian missionary tells that one day he was deeply discouraged. The uncleanness of his heart caused the work which he was conducting to be unsuccessful.

As he stood on the road considering his unworthiness and sin, he was aware of some muddy water at his feet.

«That muddy water resembles my heart,» he said to himself. «My soul is unclean and dirty.»

Lifting up his eyes, the missionary looked out over the white Himalaya mountains. The snow was glistening wonderfully in the sunshine.

«But my soul ought to be just as white and clean as that snow,» he thought.

Then suddenly an idea struck him:

«And so this muddy pool may be clean. When the sun shines, the dirty water will evaporate. It will rise again up to the clouds and be carried far away over the mountains. There it will fall as white snow.»

A gleam of joy lit up the face of the missionary.

«My soul may also become as clean as that, but in order that this may happen, I must die, and my self-life must evaporate. Then the sun of God's grace will carry me up to higher ground, and make me as white as snow. God grant me the will to put my ego to death.»

*

The poem of the day

Utterly abandoned to the Holy Ghost!
Oh! the sinking, sinking, until self is lost!
Until the emptied vessel lies broken at His Feet;
Waiting till His filling shall make the work
                                        complete.

Utterly abandoned to the will of God;
Seeking for no other path than my Master trod;
Leaving ease and pleasure, making Him my choice,
Waiting for His guidance, listening for His Voice.

Utterly abandoned! no will of my own;
For time and for eternity, His, and His alone;
All my plans and purposes lost in His sweet will,
Having nothing, yet in Him all things
                                        possessing still.

Utterly abandoned! 'tis so sweet to be
Captive in His bonds of love, yet so wondrous free;
Free from sin's entanglements, free from doubt
                                        and fear,
Free from every worry, burden, grief or care.

In the evening

Howbeit what things were gain to me, these have I counted loss for Christ. Yea verily, and I count all things to be loss for the excellency of the know-ledge of Christ Jesus my Lord, and do count them but refuse, that I may gain Christ. Phil. 3:7/8.

In order to gain Christ, you have to count all things to be loss. The more you lose the things which are gain to you, the greater richness you will get·in Christ. Compared with the righteousness of Christ, all earthly values will fade.

Do not get discouraged feeling your poverty. That is the way you are obliged to go. Thereby you will obtain the richness in God.

Everything that is yours, is but refuse. Well, but everything coming from Him, is gain.

Then you are rich and happy anyway.

Lie down quietly to sleep in the Name of Jesus. Even if you feel poor, you are rich and blessed in Him.

WITHOUT APPREHENSION

In the morning

> *Fear thou not, for I am with thee; be not dismayed, for I am thy God; I will strengthen thee; yea, I will help thee; yea, I will uphold thee with the right hand of My righteousness.* Isa. 41:10.

Dear sick friend, be not dismayed. There is no reason for it. All the promises of God are yours.

It is easy to understand that you may be dismayed and discouraged. It is the result of your sickness. Considering your own circumstances, feeling how weak and helpless you are, and looking around at this violent and rough world is enough to make both healthy and sick people frightened. But the Lord says:

«Do not look around. It is looking around that makes you dismayed.»

And so He gives two reasons for not being frightened:

«*I am with thee.*»

«*I am thy God.*»

Consider what those two assurances contain. He — the Almighty One — is your God. And He is with you, — there in your bed. He is closer to you than the one who daily nurses you.

And even He is «nursing you». He says so with three wonderful expressions:

«*I will strengthen thee.*»

«*I will help thee.*»

«*I will uphold thee.*»

What would you have been like if He had forsaken you? You would have been a poor outcast.

Until to-day He has been upholding you. And whatever may happen in the days to come, He will uphold you with the right hand of His righteousness.

At noon

«What is apprehension?» Kierkegaard asks.

And he gives this answer:

«It is tomorrow.»

An allegory tells of a man who was walking on a road, carrying a great sack on his back. He dragged on, very tired.

Then he met an Angel who stopped him.

«My friend, what are you carrying?»

«It is my cares and sorrows. Please help me to carry my heavy burden.»

«Put it down. Let us look in it,» the Angel said.

After some hesitation the man put down his sack. Though it was very heavy, the man seemed reluctant to obey.

«There are two cares that especially burden me,» the man continued. «The one concerns yesterday, and the other one tomorrow.»

Smiling, the Angel answered:

«Look! Your sack is empty! Yesterday is ended; it does not exist any more. Tomorrow has not come yet. Dear friend, go on cheerfully, but leave your empty sack here. To-day God will help you.»

The poem of the day

Yes, leave it with Him,
The lilies all do,
And they grow —

They grow in the rain,
And they grow in the dew —
Yes, they grow:
They grow in the sunshine, revealed by the light —
They grow in the darkness, all hid in the night —
Still they grow.

Yes, leave it with Him,
'Tis more dear to His heart,
You will know,
Than the lilies that bloom,
Or the flowers that start
'Neath the snow:
Whatever you need, if you seek it in prayer,
You can leave it with Him — for you are His care.
You, you know.

In the evening

Therefore let us also, seeing we are compassed about with so great a cloud of witnesses, lay aside every weight, and the sin which doth so easily beset us, and let us run with patience the race that is set before us.

For consider Him that hath endured such gain-

saying of sinners against Himself, that ye wax not weary, fainting in your souls. Heb. 12:1;3.

This Bible passage gives three rules which will save you from being tired and discouraged.

1). Lay aside every weight!

Note: every weight, – sin and everything else.

2). Consider Him! Do not look at your own sorrows and cares. Consider Him!

3). Run your race with patience. God has chosen the way you are to go, and that is the best one for you. So, be patient.

Now, lie down to sleep confidently. You have no weight any more. By faith you have left it all at the feet of Jesus. You are free.

Goodnight, in the Name of Jesus.

THE UNCHANGEABLE GOD

In the morning

> *«I am the Lord, I change not.»* Mal. 3:6.

Many things have changed recently in your life.
Your present conditions are not quite the
same as they used to be. Several things which you
used to enjoy you now miss. You are living mainly
in your memories at present, trying to put aside
all thought of the future.

In all these circumstances you yourself are changing. You are not the same person as you used to be.
Other people have seen it, and you feel it yourself.

But listen to the word given to-day:

«I, The Lord, change not.»

God is the unchangeable fact in your life. His
love for you is just as personal and heart-felt as
ever.

God is the hidden cause of every change in your
life. Nothing happens by chance, for God Himself
does not change.

His love is the same. He cares for you just as much as He did when you were a child. He will forgive your sins as He did before. His power is as great as ever, and He is ready to answer your prayers to-day as in the past.

You are changing; God is unchangeable. He will renew your spiritual life, once more giving you strength and joy.

«*I, The Lord, change not.*»

At noon

A young mother had experienced salvation in Christ. Peace and joy filled her heart. The home was enlightened by the sunshine of God. The one who enjoyed what had happened to mother most of all was little Mary. Mother sang, and Mary sang.

But after some time, the mother's song ended. It didn't matter how good and kind Mary was, her mother seemed to be just as discouraged. Frequently the child heard her mother sighing.

One day when the mother was in the barn milking, Mary saw that she looked deeply distressed. She noticed tears in her eyes.

Then the child got an idea. She ran into the kitchen and found the family Bible. Mary had noticed how often her mother read the Bible during her time of happiness. Lately, this book had been almost neglected.

Now Mary took the Bible in her arms, and hurried out to the barn. Mother sat milking when Mary entered, so she handed the Bible to her mother, saying:

«Mother, read here! It is still written there, just the same.»

Then mother arose, put her pail aside, took the Bible and Mary in her arms and said:

«Thank you, my little girl. You have comforted me. Why do I grieve? It is still written there. That is my comfort and I ought to be very glad indeed. The promises of God change not.»

The poem of the day

Don't let the song go out of your life
Though it chance sometimes to flow
In a minor strain;
It will blend again
With the major tone you know.

Don't let the song go out of your life;
Though the voice may have lost its trill,
Though the tremulous note
May die in your throat,
Let it sing in your spirit still.

Don't let the song go out of your life;
Let it ring in the soul while here;
And when you go hence,
'Twill follow you thence,
And live on in another sphere.

In the evening

The mountains may depart, and the hills be removed; but My lovingkindness shall not depart from thee, neither shall My covenant of peace be removed, saith the Lord that hath mercy on thee.
Is. 54:10.

Dear child of God, how confident you may feel!

Look at the mountains, how firmly they stand. They have stood in the same place for centuries. Not till the last fire destroys the world will they depart.

More firm even than the mountains is the lovingkindness of God. The covenant of His peace shall not be removed. Neither on the last day of judgment will He forsake you. Even if the mountains depart and the hills remove, the loving-kindness of God shall not depart, He says. Nothing is so firm and unchangeable as the covenant of His peace.

Then put away every kind of apprehension and restlessness. Be quiet and confident, and go to sleep in the secure certainly of God's kindness and mercy.

FORGIVENESS OF SINS

In the morning

> Son, be of good cheer; thy sins are for-
> given.   Matt. 9:2.

These words are spoken to a man who is ill, and these are the *first* words Jesus said to him. Later on, He heals his body; but first He forgives his sins.

Forgiveness of sins is the greatest need of every man.

What is sickness, pain and disappointment compared with the fact that I have committed sin against God? And for all my sins I have to give account before the Lord.

If I really recognize this, my sense of need will become great. True and righteous are His judgements.

Then how wonderful are the words of Jesus to every penitent sinner who dares to come to Him:

«Thy sins are forgiven.»

Dear friend, you who are ill, both bodily and spiritually, to-day Jesus greets you, saying:

«Thy sins are forgiven.» Thy sins do not exist any more.

For Jesus' sake, God is looking upon your sins as not being committed. You are pardoned. God will never call you to account for your sins, — whatever they are. Your sin is forgiven, — totally — and forever. Not even an upbraiding is left in the heart of God. For Jesus' sake He is well pleased with you.

Blessed soul! Be of good cheer! In the whole of existence, there is nothing like the forgiveness of sins.

Recognizing this, it is not so hard even to be ill. You are resting under the grace and love of God.

At noon

«Sin is our greatest affliction; forgiveness of sins our greatest joy. Sin is hell; the forgiveness of sins is Heaven.» (Scriver).

«No fire consumes the straw so quickly, as the

grace of God and the blood of Jesus does away with our sins.» (Scriver).

«Even if thy sin fills up all the world, the righteousness of Jesus is surely greater.» (Arndt).

«Grace and peace contain all of Christianity. Grace forgives sin, and peace gives the conscience rest. There is no peace of conscience without the forgiveness of sins. But sin is forgiven and taken away by grace.» (Luther).

«To forgive is different from excusing. God does not excuse sin, but He forgives it. Forgiveness contains pure grace.» (Rosenius).

«Take the forgiveness of sins out of the Christian's heart and you have taken the heart out of the Christian faith.» (H. S. Stub).

But we must always remember: there is no forgiveness without repentance and conversion.

«Some people like to trust the grace of God without being converted. Those people are deceiving themselves and are trusting the forgiveness of sins in vain.» (Scriver).

Come now, and let us reason together, saith the Lord: though your sins be as scarlet, they shall be as white as snow; though they be red like crimson, they shall be as wool. Is. 1: 18.

The poem of the day

Thou, O Christ, art all I want,
More than all in Thee I find.
Raise the fallen, cheer the faint,
Heal the sick, and lead the blind.
Just and holy is Thy name,
I am all unrighteousness
Vile and full of sin I am
Thou art full of truth and grace.

In the evening

There is therefore now no condemnation to them that are in Christ Jesus. For the law of the Spirit of life in Christ Jesus made me free from the law of sin and of death. For what the law could not do, in that it was weak through the flesh, God, sending His own Son in the likeness of sinful flesh and for sin, condemned sin in the flesh. Rom. 8:1/3.

Here is the foundation of your salvation:

What the law could not do, God did.

It is not what you have done that brings you perdition, and it is not what you ought to do that will give you righteousness. What God has done for you in Christ is your salvation.

On that account, these words are spoken to everyone who seeks the righteousness in Christ:

«Therefore there is now no condemnation to them that are in Christ Jesus.»

Your sin is forgiven. Don't let it frighten and accuse you any longer. In Christ you are clean.

Give thanks to God for the forgiveness of your sin, and then go to sleep securely. You are resting in the grace of God.

LIKE THE SPARROW

In the morning

> *Are not five sparrows sold for two*
> *pence? and not one of them is forgotten*
> *in the sight of God. But the very hairs*
> *of you head are all numbered. Fear not:*
> *ye are of more value than many spar-*
> *rows.* Luke 12:6/7.

Sparrows are not of great value. Nowadays we would not even pay two cents for five sparrows. In any case we would not take the trouble to catch them.

We do not think much of a sparrow. Of all the birds, the sparrow is the one we respect least, — that dusty little thing which is hopping at our feet. But God cares for the sparrow.

«*Not one of them is forgotten in the sight of God.*»

The many, many millions of sparrows all over the world, are included in the heart of God for daily care and love. One by one He thinks of them.

«*Not one of them is forgotten in the sight of God.*»

Then what about a human being?

«*Fear not, ye are of more value than many sparrows.*»

How many sparrows make up the value of a man?

Nobody can tell.

Neither can anyone tell how deep and warm is the love and care of God for His dear children here on earth.

The smallest thing He knows. Even the hairs of the head are all numbered. Nothing that concerns His child, He counts a trifle. Nothing is so insignificant as not to make Him care. Nothing is so small as to be out of reach of His helping hand.

Then the child of God may be confident, reliant and glad. God the Father will take care of him.

*

At noon

«Here I will make my nest,» the little bird twittered, sitting in the top of a tree, looking around on the green meadows. «What a view my young ones will get, peeping out of the nest.»

But then the bird suddenly grew silent. Far up in the air a hawk was eagerly watching the top of the tree.

Then the bird hid itself in a bush.

«I will make my nest here,» it twittered, looking around. «My young ones will be safe here.»

Then it kept quiet, listening. Some steps approached, and the branches were pushed aside by the hands of a little child.

Then the bird flew into the meadow, hiding itself in the gras.

«Oh, how beautiful,» it said. «I will build my nest here. When summer comes my young ones will be able to play here among the flowers.»

But the blades of grass were bent soundlessly, and a cat appeared. The bird had a narrow escape, and hid itself in a thorn bush.

«Well, I must build my nest here,» it sighed.

«Though the thorns prick, this is the only place where I am safe.»

And so the bird made its nest in the thorn-bush.

When summer came, the bird sat in the top of the bush and sang:

«No one has such a nice home as I have, and no one is living as safely and cosily as I. The thorns have become my best friends; they defend my young ones. And now God has covered my little home with the sweetest red roses. I thank the Lord for the thorns.»

The poem of the day

He placed me in a little cage,
Away from gardens fair;
But I must sing the sweetest songs
Because He placed me there.
Not beat my wings against the cage,
If it's my Maker's will,
But raise my voice to heaven's gate
And — sing the louder still!

*

In the evening

Yea, He loveth the people;
All His saints are in Thy hand:
And they sat down at Thy feet;
Every one shall receive of Thy words.

Deut. 33:3.

It is with these words God greets you this evening. As you are sleeping you are surrounded by the love of God. His mighty hand is your defence.

«All His saints are in Thy hand.» Even you!

You are not hidden in a lonely corner, forgotten by God and by everyone else.

«They sat down at Thy feet.» You are very close to Him, and He is looking at you with loving care. Then be calm and rest well.

YOUR FUTURE

In the morning

> *My times are in Thy hand.* Ps. 31:15.

No, it is not hopeless. Do not feel that. In sending illness to you, God has not closed your way for ever and spoiled your future. You feel you have reason to be discouraged. If it is easy to lose heart in time of health, surely you may be forgiven if life looks dark when sickness comes. But perhaps *God* blames you. Your faint-heartedness does not come from Him, and you will never be gripped by the spirit of despair unless you lose sight of your Heavenly Father.

The days of your life are in God's hands. Do not forget that. God knows all the days that lie ahead, and He decides where you are to go. God's way is always the best.

But if you are going to die, what then? We will all die one day. If you believe on Him, you have the forgiveness of sins, and God will take you to the eternal home in Heaven. Nothing is better than that, and all your dear ones can be left trustfully in God's care.

But also, in the days and the years to come, — before death — the days of your life are in the hand of God. The sun of grace and hope is shining on the whole of your future. *«For surely there is a reward; and thy hope shall not be cut off.»* Prov. 23:18.

When God closes one door, He opens another. Wait, and you will find an open door.

At noon

A little boy in the beginner's class in school was trying to learn to write with ink. He made a big blot, and then another. He put his little hand on the blots and rubbed it around, so the whole page was a dreadful sight.

With a sad face he held up his hand:

«Miss Smith, may I turn to the next page and begin again?»

Inquiring the teacher looked at him, and the boy continued:

«I have got blots on this page.»

The teacher nodded in assent.

«Yes, my boy. Turn to the next page and try again.»

We are all learning to write. Every day we write a new page in the diary of our lives. But alas, we all make blots on the pages at times. We try to remove them, and make the page look worse than ever — but, praise the Lord, — He gives us our opportunity to *beginn again*.

Do not think that everything has been spoiled for you. There is hope for your future. Soon you are going to start on a new page in your diary, and that must be a new chapter in the Name of Jesus.

The poem of the day

Is there some problem in your life to solve,
Some passage seeming full of mystery?
God knows, Who brings the hidden things to light.
He keeps the key.

Is there some door closed by the Father's Hand
Which widely opened you had hoped to see?
Trust God and wait — for when He shuts the door
He keeps the key.

Is there some earnest prayer unanswered yet,
Or answered *not* as you had thought 'twould be?
God will make clear His purpose by and by.
He keeps the key.

Have patience with your God, your patient God.
All wise, all knowing, no long-tarrier He,
And of the door of all thy future life
He keeps the key.

Unfailing comfort, sweet and blessed rest,
To know of *every* door He keeps the key.
That He at last when *He* sees 'tis best,
Will give it *Thee*.

In the evening

*And He that sitteth on the throne said: Behold,
I make all things new.* Rev. 21:5.

This is God's evening greeting to you to-night.

God will make all things new for you.

When we reach the eternal home, all things will
become new. The old things are ended. There will
be no sickness, no pain, no tears, no sin. Oh blessed
day!

But the words may refer to human life here on earth as well. God will never close your way to the future. He will make all things new for you. The new things and the new conditions He is going to give you will be much better than those of the past.

He will make the circumstances of your life new. He will make you a new person. Your faith will be renewed, — stronger and more trustful than before. Your love will become more warm, and your hope more living.

What does it matter if you have to go through tribulations, if God will make you a new and better man thereby?

YOUR PAIN

In the morning

> *And that I should not be exalted over-much, there was given to me a thorn in the flesh, a messenger of Satan to buffet me, that I should not be exalted overmuch. Concerning this thing, I besought the Lord thrice, that it might depart from me. And He hath said unto me, My grace is sufficient for thee, for My power is made perfect in weakness.*
> II Cor. 12:7/9.

Paul needed the thorn in the flesh. In love, God had to refuse his prayers.

God does not want to bring trouble to anyone. If it would benefit the children of God, no tribulations would ever come in their way.

Paul, however, was in danger of injuring his soul. He was tempted to exalt himself, therefore God had to humble him by giving him the thorn in his flesh.

If God does not consider His children to be in need of tribulation, He will not send any. But if the tribulations benefit them, they will come. The tribulations themselves are an expression of the love of God.

Even the most heartfelt prayers for escape will not make God change. He just answers:

«*My grace is sufficient for thee.*»

In not removing the messenger of Satan, God is giving a greater fullness of His grace, and always *sufficient* grace.

It is better to be small and suffering, possessing the grace of God, than to be great without pain and failing God.

«*When I am weak, then am I strong,*» Paul says.

Therefore Paul submits and accepts God's answer. In spite of the painful thorn, Paul is of good cheer. «*I take pleasure in weaknesses,*» he says.

If we accept from God the suffering we have to endure, we shall find that it is to our benefit. Receiving *sufficient grace,* we will *take pleasure* in the will of God.

*

At noon

One night poor Jacob could get nothing better than a stone as a pillow. It must have been difficult to fall asleep that night, and his sleep was disturbed and restless.

That night he had a dream. A ladder, reaching to heaven, was let down to the place where he was sleeping, and he saw the Angels of God ascending and descending on it.

He might well have felt inclined to throw the stone away, trying to find another pillow, but think what he would have lost? He would have fallen fast asleep and neither ladder nor Angels would have been revealed to him.

With his head resting on the hard stone, Jacob saw «*the gate of Heaven*». God may have given you a hard stone to rest on. You have often felt like throwing it away, but God has not allowed you to do so.

Give God thanks for your hard pillow. Released from the stone, you would have fallen fast asleep, spiritually speaking. The stone has kept you awake, consequently, you have seen the ladder which God has set up on the earth, and you have seen the Heavens opened over your head. Without knowing it you have been resting by the gate of Heaven.

Without the hard stone, your life would have missed the Angels. Now you are surrounded by the host of celestial servants who are carrying heavenly gifts to you, and carrying your prayers to the throne of God.

Let the stone be transformed into an altar. Let your sighs become praise, and your tears thanks.

> Tho' like a wanderer,
> The sun gone down,
> Darkness comes over me,
> My rest a stone ...
> Yet in my dreams I'd be
> Nearer, my God, to Thee,
> Nearer to Thee!

When the time comes, you yourself will ascend the Heavenly ladder surrounded by the singing crowd of Angels. The gate will be opened for you, and you will enter the eternal mansions to glorify God for ever.

The poem of the day

The hawthorn hedge that keeps us from intruding,
Looks very fierce and bare
When stripped by winter, every branch protruding
Thorns that would wound and tear.

But spring-time comes; and like the rod that
                                        budded,
Each twig breaks out in green;
And cushions soft of tender leaves are studded,
Where spines alone are seen.

The sorrows that to us seem so perplexing,
Are mercies kindly sent,
To guard our wayward souls from sadder vexing,
And greater ills prevent.

To save us from the pit, no screen of roses
Would serve for our defence,
The hindrance that completely interposes
Stings back like thorny fence.

Then let us sing, our guarded way thus wending,
Life's hidden snares among,
Of mercy and of judgment sweetly blending;
Earth's sad, but lovely song.

In the evening

And in that day thou shalt say, I will give thanks unto Thee, O Lord; for though Thou wast angry with me, Thine anger is turned away, and Thou comfortest me. Behold, God is my salvation; I will trust, and will not be afraid: for the Lord Jehovah, is my strength and song; and He is become my salvation. Is. 12:1/2.

Even that which appears to you as the anger of God, is actually but grace. Therefore you are to give thanks even for «the anger».

The day is coming when He will comfort you. As soon as you learn to appreciate the chastisement of God you will be consoled accordingly.

Knowing that even «the anger» actually is but grace, it will not be so difficult to glorify Him.

Try this evening to give thanks unto God. Lie down to rest in the arms of Jesus, and He will give you a good night.

„THOU ART MINE"

In the morning

> *I have called thee by thy name; thou
> art Mine.*   Is. 43:1.

God loves the whole of mankind, but He does
not love them as a multitude; He gives His
love to individuals.

It is wonderfull to know that God loves the
whole human race, — all men. «God so loved the
world . . .»

The love of God is personal. He calls us by our
name, — one by one.

Love does not get its real meaning until it reaches
the individual. Love desires contact. This contact
being made, love may develop.

Do not feel just one in a big multitude whom
God loves as a whole.

It is you whom God loves. In the great crowd of
people, the eye of God is looking for you, and this

81

divine love gets no rest until it finds you and possesses you.

The desire of His heart is to be able to say:

«*I have called thee by thy name; thou art Mine.*»

Thy name is not insignificant to Him. In His eyes you do not belong to the unknown crowd of people whose names are known to nobody.

He calls you by name. He does love you and He is eager to say: *Thou art Mine.*

He wants to communicate with you in love. He needs your confidence. He will take part in your pleasures and in your sorrows. He will carry your burdens.

And so He will whisper into your ear:

«Thou art Mine.»

At noon

Some years ago I was out flying with a friend of mine in New York who had a private plane. We had been away the whole of the day, and returned in the evening at sunset. It was a beautiful view, looking down on the great buildings, shining in the splendour of the setting sun.

Then I heard my friend singing a song about God

Who, from His Heavenly heights, is looking down on every human being. Not even the smallest child nor the blackest sinner is hidden from the divine Eye.

Once more I looked down. Realizing that far down below, eight million people were living, I was filled with strange feelings. In the great multitude down there, many lonely people whom nobody knew were living. They are without relatives and friends. They had to struggle alone for their existence. Once dead, no one would ask for them. As a pastor in New York, I had seen some examples of that.

Then the song my friend was singing came home to me. From the heights of Heaven God is looking down. He knows every human being individually; He loves everyone, and every day He is following them with His divine Eye. No suffering, no struggle, no loss, no tears are unknown to Him. He is looking for His lost sheep, and He is waiting for the prodigal son.

The divine Eye is even watching over you. He knows your pleasures and your sufferings. Nothing is foreign to Him. He calls you by your name; you are not forgotten by Him, and He knows everything about you.

The poem of the day

> Said the Robin to the Sparrow:
> «I should really like to know
> Why these anxious human beings
> Rush about and worry so?»
>
> Said the Sparrow to the Robin:
> «Friend, I think that it must be
> That they have no Heavenly Father
> Such as cares for you and me.»

In the evening

The Lord is my Shepherd; I shall not want.
He makes me to lie down in green pastures;
He leadeth me beside still waters.
He restoreth my soul:
He guideth me in the path of righteousness for
His Name's sake.
Yea, though I walk through the valley of the
shadow of death, I will fear no evil; for Thou art
with me;

Thy rod and Thy staff, they comfort me.

Thou preparest a table before me in the presence of mine enemies:

Thou hast anointed my head with oil;

My cup runneth over.

Surely goodness and lovingkindness shall follow me all the days of my life;

And I shall dwell in the house of Jehovah for ever. Psalm 23.

It may be in the evening,
When the work of the day is done,
And you have time to sit in the twilight,
And watch the sinking sun,
While the long bright day dies slowly
Over the sea,
And the hours grow quiet and holy
With thoughts of Me;
While you hear the village children
Passing along the street —
Among those passing footsteps
May come the sound of His Feet.
Therefore I tell you, Watch!
By the light of the evening star
When the room is growing dusky

As the clouds afar,
Let the door be on the latch
In your home,
For itmay be through the gloaming
I will come.

REST IN THE LORD

In the morning

> *Rest in the Lord, and wait patiently for Him.* Ps. 37:7.
> *My soul waiteth in silence for God only: from Him cometh my salvation.*
> Ps. 62:1.

It is strange that it is so difficult to rest and to become quiet.

It is difficult when we are well. The bustle of the day turns the mind outwards, and makes it restless.

We think it would be easier if we were ill, but it is still difficult.

We say that a sick person is taken aside. Nevertheless it is no simple matter really to relax, — to forget the world around you. We cannot rid ourselves of anxiety and care.

Indeed, illness itself makes us restless, and we become anxious and excited very easily.

How do we learn to become quiet?

It is learned through faith. When our helplessness becomes so great that we see no way out of it, and then become aware of God's help, the soul will learn to be quiet.

As long as we are looking around for help, considering all the possibilities, our minds will be restless and anxious.

When faith clings to God alone, the soul becomes quiet.

«From Him cometh my salvation.»

In Him you may rest. Your soul will not be disquieted any more. Centring around God alone you will find rest.

«Rest in Jehovah»!

«My soul waiteth in silence for God only.»

Trusting God, you will never be disappointed. Help will appear when God sees that the time has come. Meanwhile, He is giving the one who prays wonderfull strength and peace. The soul may relax and rest.

*

At noon

The home was poor. The mother, however, worked indefatigably, trying to keep up heart and to encourage the children.

Yet once in a while she lost heart and was discouraged.

One night she did some sewing. She was trying to make a pair of trousers for one of the boys out of some old material.

While sewing, her tears were dropping. The children were asleep and it was very late.

Only the father was awake.

«What are you weeping for, Mother?» he asked tenderly.

«I am thinking of the winter,» the mother answered. «The children have hardly any clothes.»

«What are you sewing?»

«I am trying to make some trousers for Will. He has only rags left.»

«Poor boy, then he must be very worried. Does he know that you are sewing?»

«No; Will trusts me, you know. He has no worries.»

«Well, he trusts you, therefore he is quiet and confident. We'd better learn to trust God, Mother. Then, like our boy, we shall be without cares. God never fails. Prove God, Mother.»

The poem of the day

I laid it down in silence,
This work of mine.
And took what had been sent me —
A resting time.
The Master's Voice had called me
To rest apart;
«Apart with Jesus only,»
Echoed my heart.

I took the rest and stillness
From His own Hand,
And felt this present illness
Was what He planned.
How often we choose labour,
When He says, «Rest» —
Our ways are blind and crocked;
His way is best.

The work Himself has given,
He will complete.
There may be other errands
For tired feet;
There may be other duties
For tired hands,
The present, is obedience
To His commands.

There is a blessed resting
In lying still,
In letting His Hand mould us,
Just as He will.
His work must be completed.
His lesson set;
He is the higher Workman:
Do not forget!

In the evening

The Lord is my light and my salvation; whom shall I fear? The Lord is the strength of my life; Of whom shall I be afraid? When evil-doers came upon me to eat up my flesh, even mine adversaries and my foes, they stumpled and fell.

Though a host should encamp against me, my heart shall not fear: though war should rise against me, even then will I be confident.

For in the day of trouble He will keep me secretly in His pavilion: In the covert of His tabernacle will He hide me; He will lift me up upon a rock. Ps. 27:1/3;5.

God is not only like a refuge room into which we run when the siren sounds, and which we leave again when danger is over. God is like a home where we are to live.

But God is also a refuge room. He has promised to hide us in His pavilion in time of trouble.

To this secure pavilion of His we can always have recourse. There we shall be protected and shall find confidence. There we shall learn to know the warmth of His love and the protection of His strength. No evil is able to destroy the pavilion of God.

You can trust in that, and so you can sleep confidently in the Name of Jesus.

STRONG IN WEAKNESS

In the morning

> *We have this treasure in earthen vessels,*
> *that the exceeding greatness of the power*
> *may be of God and not from ourselves.*
> II Cor. 4:7.

While you have been ill you have probably learned to acknowledge, that your body is an earthen vessel.

An earthen vessel is fragile. Even a slight shock is enough to smash the vessel to pieces.

Often we are inclined to reason very differently. We say that God should have put His treasure in a stronger and more costly vessel. A golden case would seem to us a more fitting home.

Because the earthen vessel is so frail you may be tempted to doubt whether the treasure is really in your possession. In time of illness men and women may be so conscious of their own weakness and spiritual poverty that they lose their confidence and doubt the reality of their possession of the riches of God.

Yet, this treasure is indeed yours — God has determined that His precious treasure shall be hidden in the poor vessel of your life. It is the treasure that matters — had God entrusted His riches to golden vessels, the treasure would often be forgotten as men gazed at the case that holds it.

Despite your weakness, rejoice! You possess a priceless treasure. All the riches of God are yours.

God puts His treasure in an earthen vessel that:

«The exceeding greatness of the power may be of God and not from ourselves.»

All that God asks of the vessel is that it shall be at His disposal.

God knows your weakness, and He will give you power, exceedingly great power; the power shall be of God and not of yourself.

*

The poem of the day

«He sat by a fire of seven-fold heat,
As He watched by the precious ore,
And closer He bent with a searching gaze
As He heated it more and more.
He knew He had ore that could stand the test,
And He wanted the finest gold
To mould as a crown for the King to wear,
Set with gems with a price untold.
So He laid our gold in the burning fire,
Tho' we fain would have said Him, «Nay,»
And He watched the dross that we had not seen,
And it melted and passed away.
And the gold grew brighter and yet more bright,
But our eyes were so dim with tears,
We saw but the fire — not the Master's Hand,
And questioned with anxious fears.
Yet our gold shone out with a richer glow,
As it mirrored a Form above,
That bent o'er the fire, tho' unseen by us,
With a look of ineffable love.
Can we think that it pleases His loving Heart
To cause us a moment's pain?
Ah, no! but He saw through the present cross

The bliss of eternal gain.
So He waited there with a watchful eye,
With a love that is strong and sure,
And His gold did not suffer a bit more heat,
Than was needed to make it pure.»

In the evening

*For behold your calling, brethren, that not many
wise after the flesh, not many mighty, not many
noble, are called: but God chose the foolish things
of the world, that He might put to shame them
that are wise; and God chose the weak things of
the world, that He might put to shame the things
that are strong; and the base things of the world,
and the things that are despised, did God choose,
yea and the things that are not, that He might
bring to nought the things that are: that no flesh
should glory before God. I Cor. 1:26/29.*

To-night, my soul, be still and sleep;
The storms are raging on God's deep —
God's deep, not thine; be still and sleep.

To-night, my soul, be still and sleep;
God's Hands shall still the tempter's sweep —
God's Hands, not thine; be still and sleep.

To-night, my soul, be still and sleep;
God's love is strong while night hours creep —
God's love, not thine; be still and sleep.

To-night, my soul, be still and sleep;
God's Heaven will comfort those who weep —
God's Heaven, not thine; be still and sleep.

FAITHFUL SAYING

In the morning

> *Faithful is the saying, and worthy of all acceptation, that Christ Jesus came into the world to save sinners; of whom I am chief.* I Tim. 1:15.

Here we have «*a faithful saying*», — words which every man can trust fully, — none can justly doubt their truth.

And the words are «*worthy of all acceptation*». These words are to be accepted, otherwise they have no validity for the one who hears or reads them. But every individual who accepts this message from God may rely upon them with complete confidence.

And the words are these: —

«*Christ Jesus came into the world to save sinners.*»

«For God sent not the Son into the world to judge the world; but that the world should be saved through Him.» John 3:17.

Christ has not come to punish men, nor to destroy them, nor to command fire to come down from Heaven to consume them, but Christ has come to save them.

What do you think Jesus will do concerning you? He will not condemn you, — nor punish you, — nor destroy you, — but He will *save* you!

He does not want to condemn even the greatest sinner. His whole desire is to save.

But the man who does not believe in Him and His work is already condemned. Will you not be among those who believe in Him?

This is «the faithful saying», this is indeed «worthy of all acceptation». He has come into the world to save sinners. He will save *you — to-day!*

At noon

A story is told of George Müller, the founder of several children's homes in England.

A little boy came up to him in a London street and said:

«Can't you get me into one of your children's homes, Sir?»

The boy was poor and ragged, and Müller saw that he did indeed need care and help.

«Yes, my boy, I think it can be managed. Now just go home and get some one to write a testimonial for you, telling who you are and what your circumstances are. Then come to my office tomorrow, and we will see about helping you.»

But the boy answered sadly:

«A testimonial? I do not know anyone who can write such a thing. My mother is gone; I have never known my father. I have no brothers and sisters, and I do not know anyone who can write a testimonial for me.»

His eyes were full of tears, but, taking courage, he looked imploringly at Mr. Müller and said:

«What about these rags, Sir? Aren't they enough testimonial?»

Much moved, Mr. Müller drew the boy to him, and said with a kind smile:

«Yes, my boy, your rags are testimonial enough. Come along with me.»

Jesus says:

«Him that cometh to Me, I will in no wise cast out.» John 6:37.

The poem of the day

Just as I am — without one plea,
But that Thy blood was shed for me,
And that Thou bidd'st me come to Thee,
O Lamb of God, I come.

Just as I am — and waiting not
To rid my soul of one dark blot;
To Thee whose blood can cleanse each spot,
O Lamb of God, I come.

Just as I am — Thou wilt receive,
Will welcome, pardon, cleanse, relieve;
Because Thy promise I believe,
O Lamb of God, I come.

Just as I am — Thy love unknown
Has broken every barrier down:
Now, to be Thine, yea, Thine alone,
O Lamb of God, I come.

*

In the evening

Come now, and let us reason together, saith the Lord: though your sins be as scarlet, they shall be as white as snow; though they be red like crimson, they shall be as wool. Is. 1:18.

The Lord says to mankind:

«Come now, and let us reason together.»

God calls you to a kind of trial, a strange trial indeed:

You are the accused, He is the Accuser. He wants to bring your sin into the light. He asks but one thing of you: that you shall plead guilty, admitting your sin.

If you do so, He will forgive you. The accused will be pardoned. The Judge Himself will become your Advocate. The verdict of acquittal is not conditional.

In spite of the fact that the guilt is quite plain, He will temper justice with mercy. Your hideous sin shall become white as snow. You shall be cleansed.

And so the question is:

Do you dare to reason with Him?

UNDER THE WINGS OF GOD

In the morning

> *He will cover thee with His pinions, and under His wings shalt thou take refuge: His truth is a shield and a buckler.*
>
> Ps. 91:4.

Here we are given a beautiful illustration of God's relation to His children: the picture of a bird protecting its young.

When the mother bird becomes aware of danger, she flies at once to the nest and covers the little ones with her body and wings to protect them.

The fledglings themselves know nothing of this danger. They only feel the warm wings of their mother and hear the throbbing of her heart and so they fall asleep in safety.

The parent bird thinks only of her young. She lives only for their benefit, working for them all day long. As long as their mother is alive, the baby birds will be well cared for and will lack nothing.

When evening comes, under the wings of their mother, close to her warm breast, sheltered from the cold, the young birds sleep securely and without anxiety.

Even if the mother is small, and the young ones are many, there is always room for all. The spread of the wings is just as wide as her love.

In the Bible-words for to-day we read:

«He will cover thee with His pinions, and under His wings shalt thou take refuge.»

Under the wings of God, there is room for all of us, and no one need stay outside.

When anxiety comes, we may hide ourselves under His wings. If we keep very quiet, we will be able to hear the very throbbing of His tender Heart.

A cruel hand may throw a bird away and destroy the nest, but those who are resting under the wings of Almighty God are beyond the reach of men.

«He will cover thee with His pinions.»

At noon

A little boy accompanied his father on a visit far out into the country.

On their way, they had to pass a small bridge

which had no railing. The current of the river underneath was very strong. The boy got frightened, and his father had to help him to cross the bridge.

After that, the boy's enjoyment of the trip was gone. In the home of the friends whom they were visiting, the boy again and again asked his father:

«Dad, aren't we going home soon? It is getting dark. Don't forget the bridge.»

The father could not leave so soon, and the boy started to cry. Eventually, he cried himself to sleep.

In the evening the father took the sleeping child in his arms and carried him home.

As he was being put to bed, the boy awoke, and, looking around, asked:

«Where am I?»

«You are at home,» the father answered.

«But the bridge, Dad, — that dangerous bridge?»

Smiling the father patted his head, saying:

«That dangerous bridge . . . ? You were sleeping, my boy, and so I carried you home in my arms.»

In human experience there are many torrential rivers to cross by bridges which seem dangerously slender. May we all learn not to dread in advance what may happen.

God Himself has promised to carry us in His strong Arms.

At last, He will carry us over the River of Death, while we are sleeping securely.

The poem of the day

When thou passest through the waters
Deep the waves may be and cold,
But Jehovah is our refuge,
And His promise is our hold;
For the Lord Himself hath said it,
He, the faithful God and true;
«When thou comest to the waters
Thou shalt not go down, *but through.*»

Seas of sorrow, seas of trial,
Bitterest anguish, fiercest pain,
Rolling surges of temptation,
Sweeping over heart and brain —
They shall never overflow us
For we know His Word is true;
All His waves and all His billow
He will lead us safely through.

Threatening breakers of destruction,
Doubt's insidious undertow,
Shall not sink us, shall not drag us
Out to ocean depths of woe;
For His promise shall sustain us,
Praise the Lord, whose Words is true!
We shall not go down, or under,
For He saith, «Thou passest *through.*»

In the evening

But Zion said, the Lord hath forsaken me, and the Lord hath forgotten me. Can a woman forget her sucking child, that she should not have compassion on the son of her womb? yea, these may forget, yet will not I forget thee. Behold, I have graven thee upon the palms of My hands; thy walls are continually before me. Is. 49:14/16.

A mother does not forget her child; just because she is the mother and the child belongs to her.

God does not forget you, just because He is God and you belong to Him.

The babe at the breast is entirely dependent on the mother. In like manner you are dependent on

God. Your future and your whole being are given over to His care.

It is the nature of a mother to care for her child. She *must* do it because she is the mother, loving her child.

And so it is in accordance to the nature of God that He cares for you. He *must* do it, because He is God, your Father, Who loves His child with a perfect love.

THE BROKEN HEART

In the morning

> *A bruised reed will He not break.*
> Is. 42:3.

The one who is ill may often feel useless and set aside.

He feels like a reed that is bruised. The illness broke him, and so he is put aside as unserviceable.

Yet life goes on, and around him everything continues as it used to do — he alone is neglected.

Others are working, are rejoicing, — without him. He is like a broken, useless reed.

In time of illness this is one of the hardest lessons to learn, that life around him is continuing undisturbed, even when he is set aside. No man is indispensable.

Through this experience the child of God must learn how necessary it is to be humble.

But no one is to despise himself on that account.

Even if in your own eyes you are only a bruised reed, God is watching over you in love, and you are precious in His sight.

«*A bruised reed He shall not break.*»

God does not despise you. He has not neglected you, nor has He thrown you away to be trampled down and bruised.

«*He will bring forth justice in truth.*» Is. 42:3.

He will heal the reed which is bruised. He will make it stronger, better and more useful.

Only wait for Him.

At noon

One day a famous violinist entered a music shop to buy a violin.

«Let me try the best instrument you have,» he said.

The shop-keeper gave him one.

And the artist played.

But after a few strokes with the bow, he flew into a rage. Throwing the violin away, he left the shop.

«How can you offer me a thing like that?» he exclaimed as he went out.

Left alone, the music-seller took up the violin and found it smashed to pieces. He picked up the fragments, entered his workshop, and there with skilled hands he fitted the pieces of the violin together.

Some time later, the violinist returned. The seller gave him the same violin.

Taking it, he started to play and was amazed at the beauty of the tones drawn from the violin. The artist forgot time and place, and could hardly cease playing.

After a while he put the violin down.

«This is a masterpiece, something quite out of the ordinary,» he exclaimed. «Where did you discover such a fine instrument?»

Smiling, the seller answered:

«You have played on that same violin once before. Then you flew into a rage and smashed it. Now I have fitted the pieces together, and there is the violin.»

Perhaps this is what God is doing with you.

The tones of your instrument may be too harsh. Therefore God has to break it to pieces. You have been going through painful times.

111

God will not leave you there. Carefully He is fitting together the pieces of your instrument. One day He will start to play on it again, and then He will draw out nobler music with a new depth and tenderness in its tones.

The poem of the day

«They tell me I must bruise
The rose's leaf,
Ere I can keep and use
Its fragrance brief.

They tell me I must break
The skylark's heart,
Ere her cage song will make
The silence start.

They tell me love must bleed,
And friendship weep,
Ere in my deepest need
I touch that deep.

Must it be always so
With precious things?

Must they be bruised and go
With beaten wings?

Ah, yes! By crushing days,
By caging nights, by scar
Of thorn and stony ways,
These blessings are!»

In the evening

For thus saith the high and lofty One that inhabiteth eternity, Whose Name is Holy: I dwell in the high and holy place, with him also that is of a contrite and humble spirit, to revive the spirit of the humble, and to revive the heart of the contrite. Is. 57:15.

God has two places to dwell in:

1) *In the high and holy place.*

Considering this, we say: That is a worthy tabernacle for God.

2) *With him that is of a contrite and humble spirit.*

To that statement our hearts will exclaim: «Thanks be to God, the Holy and Merciful: What a miracle! Then He will dwell even in me.»

And so we will pray:

«Revive my contrite heart, renew my strength and my joy.»

That is a prayer He has promised to answer. For that purpose He makes His dwelling-place in the contrite and broken heart.

HE AND YOU

In the morning

> *I know their sorrows.* Exod. 3:7.

God knows the sorrows and sufferings of His people.

When you are suffering, God Himself knows and feels your pain.

The one who is ill, often feels lonely. Even if day by day he is surrounded by sympathy, love and helpfulness, no one else can know just how sick one really feels, both physically and spiritually.

The hidden pain of his inmost heart is something he has to carry alone. However kind and loving others may be, *he* is the one who is ill, and it is he who feels the weakness and weariness, and who suffers in mind, body and soul.

Yes, it is he, — the sick one.

Nevertheless — he is not alone.

God, the Heavenly Father says:

«*I know your sorrows.*»

God has made your sufferings His own. Your sorrows are His sorrows. Your pain is His pain. His love for you now is so great that He has entered into your condition. You never feel a pain alone; He is united with you in love. Your pleasures are His pleasures. When you weep, He Himself grieves; He is awake when you cannot sleep. He holds your hand when you are afraid. He is close to your bed when you are sleeping.

All your sufferings, your cares and your pleasures are known to God.

Once He was crowned with thorns and nailed to a cross, suffering nameless agony. And that happened to Him instead of to you. Then He demonstrated and proved His love to you. The penalty of sin was laid upon Him. And He took it freely.

Knowing that He has suffered for you on the cross, you can never doubt that He will join you in your sorrows to-day.

✳

At noon

The knowledge of the fact that Christ has suffered for mankind brings help to every one in learning how to bear his own pain with the right mind and spirit.

About this *Luther* says:

If you are oppressed by sorrow or illness, consider how insignificant it is compared with Christ's crown of thorns and the nails in His hands.

If you are to do what you do not like, consider how Christ was made a Prisoner, bound and led hither and thither.

If you are tempted to be proud, consider how your Lord was mocked and despised, reckoned with robbers.

If you are tempted to uncleanness and evil desires, remember how the pure body of Christ was whipped and scourged.

When tempted by hatred, envy and thoughts of revenge, remember how Christ with many tears prayed for you and for all His enemies, even though He had a greater right to take vengeance.

If sorrows and other kinds of adversities, bodily or spiritual, oppress you, strengthen your heart by saying: «Well, why should I not suffer a little when my Lord has sweated blood in the garden in agony and in anxiety?»

The poem of the day

The day when Jesus stood alone
And felt the hearts of men like stone,
And knew He came but to atone —
That day «He held His peace».

They witnessed falsely to His Word,
They bound Him with a cruel cord,
And mockingly proclaimed Him Lord;
«But Jesus held His peace.»

They spat upon Him in the face,
They dragged Him on from place to place,
They heaped upon Him all disgrace;
«But Jesus held His peace.»

In the evening

For we have not a high priest that cannot be touched with the feeling of our infirmities; but One that has been in all points tempted like as we are, yet without sin. Let us therefore draw near with boldness unto the throne of grace, that we may receive mercy, and may find grace to help us in time of need. Heb. 4:16/17.

Christ was tempted like as you are. Consequently:

1) He understands your temptations.

2) He is touched with the feeling of your infirmities.

3) He is able and willing to help you.

Christ does not blame you for your infirmity; He feels for you and sympathizes with you in your sorrows.

Therefore, you may boldly come unto the Throne of Grace obtaining mercy and help in time of need.

How happy you are, having such a Brother and Saviour.

AS THE FLOWER

In the morning

> *All flesh is grass and all the goodliness thereof is as the flower of the field. The grass withereth, the flower fadeth: but the word of our God shall stand for ever.* Is. 40:6;8.

Do not be proud, oh man, but fear. All flesh is grass. Of such a short duration is human life that the power of resistance is weak, and death so near. The grass withers, the flower fades.

Perhaps you have already perceived the weakness of the flesh? Then prepare yourself to meet your God.

There is one thing that is eternal: *«The Word of our God shall stand for ever.»* And consequently also the one who is regenerated by this Holy Word, and has eternal life. Live in the Word of God and you shall never «wither».

«The goodliness of men is as the flower of the field.»

Even if the life of a flower is short, it is beautiful. And its glory is from God. No man is able to make a flower.

Therefore the flower in a wonderful way is talking about the Creator. From the day of budding until the flowering season, it is telling about the glory of God.

By its beauty it gives joy to men, with its fragrance it fills the air, — always unconcerned and happy. The Creator gives sun and rain. All beauty is received from Him.

«The goodliness of men is as the flower of the field.»

All human life receives its beauty from God. Men may live a life as happy and free from anxiety as the flower. «If God doth so clothe the grass of the field, which to-day is, and to-morrow is cast into the oven, shall He not much more clothe you, O ye of little faith?» Matt. 6:30.

Like the flower we are to fill the air with fragrance, — the sweet savour of Christ. (II Cor. 2:14.)

Even if life is uncertain and short like that of the flower, it may become just as rich and beautiful.

At noon

Søren Kierkegaard tells this allegory:

A lily was growing in a lonely place. There were very few flowers there. The soil was poor, and the surroundings had no beauty. But the lily was always content and happy.

One day it happened that the lily got a good friend: a little bird. By and by the bird came to see the lily and soon they were talking together.

The bird told of the different things which it had seen as it flew around, and talked of the beauty of nature in other places.

«You ought to see the country beyond those distant hills. There is a meadow filled with the loveliest flowers and the soil is rich and good.»

The lily looked around and longed to get away. From that day it was no longer content. The surroundings appeared so ugly and empty.

One day the lily asked:

«Dear bird, my friend, please take me with you.
I can't stand being here any longer.»

And so the little bird picked the flower and
carried it over into the meadow.

And there — surrounded by all the lovely flowers
— the lily lay withering.

Many people have the fate of the lily. Therefore:
be content in the circumstances where God has
placed you.

The poem of the day

I'll stay where You've put me; I will, dear Lord.
Though I wanted so badly to go;
I was eager to march with «the rank and file»,
Yes, I wanted to lead them, You know.
I planned to keep step to the music loud,
To cheer when the banner unfurled,
To stand in the midst of the fight straight and
proud
But I'll stay where You've put me.

I'll stay where You've put me; I will, dear Lord;
I'll bear the day's burden and heat,
Always trusting Thee fully; when even has come
I'll lay heavy sheaves at Thy Feet.

And then, when my earth work is ended and done,
In the light of eternity's glow,
Life's record all closed, I surely shall find
It was better to stay than to go;
I'll stay where You've put me.

In the evening

Wherefore I take pleasure in weakness, in injuries, in necessities, in persecutions, in distresses, for Christ's sake: for when I am weak, then am I strong. II Cor. 12:10.

Do not complain, even if you feel the conditions of life are hard and yourself weak and crippled.

Your complaints will only make your suffering still worse.

Your happiness does not depend on the conditions of your life, but on you yourself. Learn of the great Apostle when he says: «*I take pleasure in my weaknesses.*» In that way the power of God will be revealed to you. «*For when you are weak, then you are strong.*»

Therefore do not be discouraged and start sorrowing. Be of good cheer, be happy in your own mind. The power of God will uphold you.

A FREE SPIRIT

In the morning

> *Uphold me with a willing spirit.*
> Ps. 51:12.

To-day you are confronted with a serious question:

Are you really *willing* to suffer? In other words, have you a *willing spirit?*

Do not take that question lightly. Many things depend on your answer. When God puts this question to you, you must reply.

Jesus Himself had to face that same question. It cost Him His hardest struggle. And the result was the greatest victory ever won. Through that victory we to-day may obtain salvation from God.

Jesus prayed:

«*Not My will but Thine, be done.*» That is the victory. Jesus was willing to suffer and consequently the whole world was saved. He gave His life with a willing Spirit.

It does not follow as a matter of course that your illness will be a blessing to you. It depends upon your attitude of mind during your illness.

The main thing is never *how much* a man suffers, but *how* he is suffering.

What God is looking for, is the humbled will. All protests against the way of God must cease. If your mind is unwilling and dissatisfied, the blessing from above will fail to come.

Even you have your Calvary where you are to bring your sacrifices. If your cross is to bring pleasure to God, you must first fight your struggle in your Gethsemane.

Humility belongs to faith. You have to submit to the will of God, recognizing that the way by which He is leading you is for your good, — even if you would have preferred to go another way. Are you able to give Him thanks even for your pain? Faith will have its greatest triumph.

The ego wants to have its own will; faith is yielding to the will of God, whatever the path may be, giving Him thanks for all things.

In this manner, suffering will be transformed into glory, and pain will get wings which lift the soul nearer to God.

At noon

Two sisters were walking along a road. The sun was shining and the scent of flowers filled the air.

After a while, however, the road became very narrow and stony. Evening came and it grew dark.

«I won't go any further,» the elder sister said. «Look at that desolate road.»

«But we must,» the other replied, «otherwise we shall not get home.»

Then two Angels appeared. Each of them sent to one of the sisters and grasped them by the hands.

The elder one resisted.

«Leave me alone,» she said weeping. «I will return. I dare not go any farther.»

The Angel, however, dragged her further. In spite of anxiety and opposition, she had to follow.

When the other sister saw the Angel, a smile spread over her face.

«Have you come to help me on my way home?» she asked.

«Yes, just take my hand. Lift your head and look forward.»

«Oh, I see a light far off.»

«That comes from your home. They are expecting you.»

Then the sister forgot the darkness, the stones and the narrow road.

«It does not matter if the way is hard and the road narrow. I am going home,» she said bravely.

Both sisters reached home, one of them resisting, suffering and complaining, the other happy, expectant and cheerful.

God grant us all a willing spirit to follow His ways, whatever they may be.

The poem of the day

O break my heart; but break it as a field
Is by the plough up-broken for the corn;
O break it as the buds, by green leaf sealed,
Are, to unloose the golden blossom, torn;
Love would I offer unto Love's great Master,
Set free the odour, break the alabaster.

O break my heart; break it victorious God,
That life's eternal well may flash abroad;
O let it break as when the captive trees,

Breaking cold bonds, regain their liberties;
And as thought's sacred grove to life is springing,
Be joys, like birds, their hope, Thy victory singing.

In the evening

*But now thus saith the Lord that created thee,
O Jacob, and He that formed thee, O Israel: Fear
not, for I have redeemed thee; I have called thee
by thy name, thou art Mine. When thou passest
through the waters, I will be with thee; and through
the rivers, they shall not overflow thee: when thou
walkest through the fire, thou shalt not be burned,
neither shall the flame kindle upon thee. Thou hast
been precious in My sight and honorable, and I have
loved thee. Is. 43:1;2;4a.*

«I will be with thee.» These words make all fear
disappear. Rivers cannot overflow — and fire cannot burn the one who trusts in God.

Therefore, be trustful and confident.

As a «good night» He whispers into your ear:
«*I will be with thee!*»

THE PRAYER OF THE POOR ONE

In the morning

> But the publican, standing afar off, would not lift up so much as his eyes unto heaven, but smote his breast, saying, God, be Thou merciful to me a sinner.   Luke 18:13.

Often we take it for granted that one who is ill, has plenty of time and strength for prayer. And often the sick one expects it of himself. When well, he was always busy, and found little time for prayer. Now, however, there ought to be plenty of time.

And yet he does not pray very much, and it is a disappointment to him. He blames himself for being spiritually indolent, and he grows anxious. He tries to pull himself together, but with little success.

And the cause is: He is too tired both bodily

and spiritually, therefore he is unable to concentrate on anything.

Dear friend, do not reproach yourself for that. Your weakness is a result of your illness.

When you are weak and ill, God does not expect you to pray long prayers.

Feeling that you are standing afar off, like the publican, not daring to lift up so much as your eyes unto Heaven, pray confidently your prayer:

«God be Thou merciful to me, a sinner.»

That is a prayer with which God is well pleased.

That prayer is always answered.

That prayer is able to save your soul.

A sigh from a penitent sinner is opening the door to the rich resources of God's grace.

Let this sigh ascend from your heart even if you feel unable to pray anything more than that. Then you are rich, even though you feel so poor. Then you are blessed, though feeling deeply distressed.

At noon

There are prayers which do not contain a single word.

1) *Weeping* may be prayer.

A sinful woman is lying at the feet of Jesus. She cannot say a single word. The weeping is choking her. The tears, however, are flowing freely, and she wipes His feet with her hair.

And this prayer without words is answered. Happy in her mind, she goes away possessing the two greatest gifts anyone may receive:

The forgiveness of sins and the peace of God.

2) *Sighs* may be prayer.

Israel was slaving in Egypt. The people are working so hard that they are unable to pray. But sighs are ascending, — thousands of painful sighs.

And God says:

«The cry of the children of Israel is come unto Me.»

In the ear of God, the *sigh* of His people has become a *cry*. And He has descended to save them.

3) *Distress* may be prayer.

Israel is standing on the shores of the Red Sea, and behind them are the strong forces of the enemy. Moses is in a state of great distress. Strangely however, it is not recorded that Moses prayed to God.

Yet God says: «Wherefore criest thou unto Me?»

And once more God saved His people.

The distress of a child of God is prayer, — even without words.

«*The Lord will fight for you, and ye shall hold your peace.*»

The poem of the day

Dear Child, God does not say today, «Be strong»;
He knows your strength is spent; He knows
                                    how long
The road has been, how weary you have grown,
For He who walked the earthly roads alone,
Eeach bogging lowland, and each rugged hill,
Can understand, and so He says, «Be Still,
And know that I am God.» The hour is late,
And you must rest awhile, and you must wait
Until life's empty reservoirs fill up
As slow rain fills an empty upturned cup.
Hold up your cup, dear child, for God to fill.
He only asks today that you be still.

*

In the evening

For all have sinned, and fall short of the glory of God; being justified freely by His grace through the redemption that is in Christ Jesus.

Romans 3:23/24.

To be righteous means to be adequate to the measures of God. The Eye of God, however, does not tolerate any fault. Consequently, none is righteous, no, not one.

Therefore, there is but one way to righteousness: *the way of grace.*

«*We are justified freely by His grace.*»

That being the case, every man may be justified. That is, every one who is humble enough to receive grace.

Even you!

By grace the perfect righteousness of Christ is reckoned to a sinner. Christ put Himself in the sinner's place. In the Eyes of God, the sinner is just as perfect as Christ is.

Can you then keep on doubting that even you stand righteous before the Face of the Lord?

OPEN YOUR WINDOWS!

In the morning

> *Daniel went into his house (now his*
> *windows were open in his chamber to-*
> *ward Jerusalem); and he kneeled upon*
> *his knees three times a day, and prayed,*
> *and gave thanks before his God, as he*
> *did aforetime.* Dan. 6:10.

You are in need of fresh air.

Open your windows!

In times of tribulation many people keep their troubles to themselves, and there, in an isolation of their own, they consider all their difficulties.

In this way their burdens grow still greater, and the air in their enclosure becomes unhealthy and heavy.

Do not that! Open your windows! Stand before the window toward Jerusalem, breathing in the healthy air that is streaming to you from above.

In front of those windows, many who have an

ill and depressed mind, have been breathing in joy and health.

To Daniel life had become difficult. The difficulties, however, made him kneel down in prayer and thanksgiving three times a day. Notice that Daniel's prayer before those windows was transformed into thanksgiving.

Jerusalem is, spiritually speaking, our native country, our heavenly home. There our love is centered, there is the place we are longing for. Jerusalem is the goal of life's journey.

Here we are strangers and foreigners. We are citizens of the Kingdom of God. Our citizenship is in Heaven.

This we are not to forget. We have to stand frequently before the open windows, looking homeward, waiting for the day of removal.

Looking toward Jerusalem will give you a heart that is centered on Heaven.

At noon

On a little island far out in the Norwegian skerries, lived a woman who had been ill for many years.

The days passed with no variation, each day was

like very other. Always the same people, the same pictures on the wall, the same bed in the same place.

The sick woman wanted it that herself. She did not like changes.

One day, however, she asked her people to move her bed.

They were surprised, but the invalid told them: «I am so exited. Something is going to happen. I can feel it. I wonder if Jesus is soon going to return? Move my bed, dear. I want to lie over there where I can look through the window — eastward. My eyes must be ready for the first glimpse of Him when He appears in the clouds, — my dear Saviour.»

May all the children of God both in life and in death, have the joyful expectation of the coming of Christ, and always be ready to leave this earth and to follow in His train.

The poem of the day

One day the trumpet will sound for His coming.
One day the skies with His glory will shine;
Wonderful day, my beloved ones bringing;
Glorious Saviour, this Jesus is mine!

In the evening

Let not your heart be troubled: believe in God, believe also in Me. In My Father's house are many mansions; if it were not so, I would have told you; for I go to prepare a place for you, I come again, and will receive you unto Myself; that where I am, there ye may be also. John 14:1/3.

What is Jesus doing now?

He is preparing a place for you in Heaven.

«Father's house», — that means: at home.

Whether the day is near or far off, in Heaven they are looking forward with pleasure and joy to your moving from earth into the Celestial Home.

On that day, everything will be prepared for you. You will at once feel at home, noticing that they all have been waiting for you to welcome you home.

Even you ought to rejoice as you consider this.

As Heaven is prepared for you, so you ought to be prepared for Heaven. Be ready to depart. Keep the garment of your soul pure, cleansed in the blood of the Lamb.